JAGUAR

A Tradition of Luxury and Style

By Paul W. Cockerham

Mason Crest
450 Parkway Drive, Suite D
Broomall, PA 19008
www.masoncrest.com

Printed and bound in the United States of America.

Series ISBN: 978-1-4222-3828-8
Hardback ISBN: 978-1-4222-3832-5
EBook ISBN: 978-1-4222-7957-1

First printing
1 3 5 7 9 8 6 4 2

Additional text by Bob Woods.

Cover photograph by NaturSports/Dreamstime.com.

Library of Congress Cataloging-in-Publication Data is on file with the publisher.

SPEED RULES!
INSIDE THE WORLD'S HOTTEST CARS

BMW

CORVETTE

FERRARI

JAGUAR

LAMBORGHINI

MERCEDES-BENZ

MUSTANG

PORSCHE

CONTENTS

KEY ICONS TO LOOK FOR

Educational Videos: Readers can view videos by scanning our QR codes, providing them with additional educational content to supplement the text. Examples include news coverage, moments in history, speeches, iconic moments, and much more!

Series Glossary of Key Terms: This back-of-the-book glossary contains terminology used throughout this series. Words found here increase the reader's ability to read and comprehend higher-level books and articles in this field.

Research Projects: Readers are pointed toward areas of further inquiry connected to each chapter. Suggestions are provided for projects that encourage deeper research and analysis.

INTRODUCTION

The automobiles of Jaguar have always been singularly beautiful creations, as well as enthusiastic performers and outstanding values. From the beginning, they appealed to a society that wanted transportation that was more appealing than Great Britain's generally pedestrian offerings, but more reasonably priced than the top–end marques such as Rolls–Royce and Bentley.

The company was launched by a pair of motorcycle enthusiasts in Blackpool, Lancashire: William Walmsley, and a young entrepreneurial fellow named William Lyons, a son of a local family whose business sense and eye for design would ultimately make Jaguar an extension of his personality and vision. With loans from their fathers, the pair established the Swallow Sidecar Company in a tiny Blackpool shop in 1922. Lyons' business savvy allowed the company to thrive, and within four years the company moved to larger quarters that allowed it to expand operations to include automotive body building and repair.

At the time, the tiny Austin Seven automobile was enjoying considerable success, which Swallow duly noted. The company bought a rolling chassis and designed and built an attractive body, launching the car in 1927 as the Austin Swallow. The car was an overnight success, with the volume of dealer orders necessitating to a 40,000-square–foot factory in Foleshill in the Midlands. Production soon rose to 50 cars per week, including production on chassis from other car companies such as Standard, Swift, and Morris.

Standard Nine and Sixteen rolling chassis would soon form the foundation for new designs from Swallow, the SS 1 and SS 2. Introduced to the public in 1931 as drophead and fixed–head coupes, the SS

The long hood and cycle wings mark this vehicle as an early–vintage (1931) SS 1. The hood ornament appears to be a one–off parody of a Rolls–Royce appendage.

Swallow's first fully original car design, the SS 1, was built on a modified chassis supplied by Standard. The long hood and rakish lines suggested speed, but it was not to be found in this car: it's six–cylinder engine developed only 16 hp.

cars had long, low lines and were as impressively equipped as cars selling for four times the money. They propelled Swallow's profits to £38,000 ($190,000) by 1934, at which time the business became a public company and Walmsley's interest was bought out by Lyons.

Lyons first applied the Jaguar name to a model with the introduction of the SS Jaguar saloon series in 1935. A six–cylinder, 2.5–litre engine that had twin carburetors and produced 103 hp powered this very sleek four–door design. Leather and woodwork graced the interior in rich abundance. Also produced were 1.5– and 3.5–litre versions, with the latter propelling the SS Jaguar to a top speed of 90 mph. By the time World War II started, 14,000 Jaguars had been produced.

At the same time, SS Cars Limited started work on its first sports cars. First was the SS 90, based on a shortened SS 1 chassis; the model was never truly promoted and only 23 units were built before it was replaced by the altogether lovely SS 100, introduced in 1935 in 2.5– and 3.5–litre versions.

During the war the company produced parts for and repaired, military aircraft, and in a return to its roots, manufactured approximately 10,000 motorcycle sidecars for the military. The sidecar business was ultimately sold in 1944.

With the war and the much publicized excesses of the Nazi period giving an unfortunate connotation to the company's "SS" initials, its name was changed to Jaguar Cars Limited in February 1945, with car production resuming that September with the resurrection of pre–war designs.

While on fire–watch duty during the war, Lyons and his engineers sketched out a design for an advanced new engine for a new postwar saloon design. Development continued in Jaguar's early days, along with work on a new chassis and front suspension. The chassis and suspension was ready by 1948, but the engine was still being developed, as was the saloon's new body, the lines of which were quite complex for steelworking. An interim model, the Mark V, debuted with the new chassis and suspension; although its lines were highly reminiscent of the SS Jaguar, the public loved it.

The new engine bowed later in the year in what had been planned as a limited–run sports car, the XK–100 (a four–cylinder vehicle) and XK–120 (six cylinders). The price differential between the two was so small the XK–100 never entered production, but the XK–120 was a sensation and the focal point for expanding the company's distribution into the lucrative United States market. It also provided a starting point for Jaguar's brief but success-ful history in sports–car racing.

The top–of–the–line saloon finally bowed in 1950 as the Mark VII, a large, lavish car fitted with the 160 hp–XK engine and the company's usual rich leather and wood trim treatments inside. Factory space at Foleshill soon became tight, so Lyons, in 1950, purchased a former Daimler factory, with one million square feet of space, in Coventry.

A new mid–sized car, the 2.4–litre saloon, was introduced in 1956, the same year William Lyons was knighted for his work in the automotive industry. A 3.4–liter model was added the following year.

These were heady days for Jaguar: its models were exemplars of style and performance, the company was profitable and growing. So when a major factory fire destroyed hundreds of cars on Feb. 12, 1957 and sus-pended production, it was indicative of the drive of Sir William Lyons and

FOLLOWING PAGE: Leftover D–types were converted into hairy XK–SS passenger cars with the addition of bumpers, convertible tops, and Ford Consul windscreens. Only 16 were made before fire swept through the Coventry works.

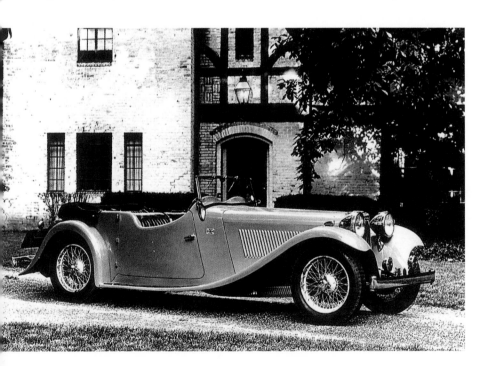

A fold–down wind-screen and cutaway doors made the SS 1 Tourer a sport-ing proposition. This is a 1935 model.

the dedication of Jaguar's workforce that production resumed within only a few days.

Growth forced another move in 1960 which resulted in the outright purchase of Daimler Car Company Limited, giving Jaguar another major factory within a couple of miles and a total workforce of over 8,000 workers. Purchases of truck manufacturer Guy Motors Limited of Wolverhampton followed in 1961, and race–engine/forklift truck–maker Coventry–Climax in 1963.

By the end of 1959 a new compact saloon, the Mark II, had been introduced, and during the 1960s it became the most popular Jaguar saloon ever, with over 92,000 produced, until the XJ series was introduced.

But the car most representative of Jaguar's heritage was the E–type sports car (also known as the XK–E), produced between 1962 and 1975. Its mystique and influence has probably never been equaled by any other production automobile.

The 1960s and 1970s saw the company continue to develop several generations of what were now known as XJ saloons in the face of economic pressures affecting the entire British automotive industry. Lyons merged Jaguar with British Motor Corporation in July 1966 to form a new conglomerate called British Motor Holdings (BMH) Limited; by 1968 he resigned as the group's managing director. BMH merged with the Leyland Group that May to form British Leyland.

A front–on view of the Mark II cat on the prowl. The grill–flanking foglamps were a distinctive feature.

On the car front, a new XJ6 was introduced in late 1968, which was voted Great Britain's Car of the Year for 1969. Three years later a V–12 engine became available; in 1972 this XJ12 was similarly honored. A controversial coupe utilizing this engine, the XJS, bowed in 1975, a design unlike anything Jaguar, or any other manufacturer, had ever produced. Despite mixed reviews, it remained in production into the 1990s.

Jaguar ceased to be a separate company in October 1972. The following 10 years saw company morale, and more importantly, build–quality, erode to desperate levels. The company started to revive early in the 1980s under the direction of John Egan, who negotiated the purchase of Jaguar's facilities to make the company fully independent and private by 1984. The company's board was confident enough to launch a new engineering, research, and development facility at Whitley. The 1987 model year saw the launch of a new XJ saloon series that helped start rebuild Jaguar's shattered reputation for build–quality.

By the early 1990s, Jaguar, with its niche market of fast, luxurious cars, represented a tasty takeover target for a larger company, and rumors swirled involving possible interest by BMW and General Motors. But it proved to be the Ford Motor Company that took over in January 1991, and the company since then has prospered with the introduction of incremental models, a major investment in new assembly capacity, and dramatic increases in performance, refinement, and build–quality.

Armed with resources equal to its distinctive legacy, Jaguar's big cats from Coventry appear poised for future prosperity.

The XJ200 boasted 500 hp and for a while was considered the fastest car on earth.

Swallow Sidecar bought a rolling chassis from Austin
of its popular and diminuitive Seven model, added stylish
bodywork, and launched Britain's first "people's car",
the Austin Swallow, in 1927. The car was an instant success.

CHAPTER ONE

BEGINNINGS

Without William Lyons there never would have been a Jaguar, for the company had his personality written all over it. Not only did he direct its operations, but also he served as chief stylist, developed more than a dozen significant automobiles, while directing engineering operations, advertising, and racing. He worked well with organized labor and the English government.

Born in Blackpool on September 4,1901, William Lyons was the son of a visiting Irish musician who never went home because he had fallen in love with a local girl known as Minnie. At the time of William's birth, the family had an established business selling pianos.

His interest in cars was germinated during an apprenticeship at Crosssley Motors Limited, and by the age of 18, he was working as a salesman at a local car dealership.

Compared to the United States and Germany, England had a relatively late start in deveoping an automotive industry, and had no popularly priced automobile for the middle class during the the pre–World War I period. Youths of the time drove motorcycles, with sidecars attached, as a means of transportation.

Lyons owned an early Harley–Davidson bike, and got to know a fellow enthusiast named William Walmsley, whose family had recently moved into the neighborhood. Walmsley was building sidecars out of his family's garage; Lyons bought one and soon proposed the pair go into sidecar manufacturing together. They waited until Lyons' twenty–first birthday, so he could obtain loans from banks, and with support from their fathers, the pair founded the Swallow Sidecar Company on September 4, 1922.

The aluminum bodied, torpedo–shaped Swallow sidecars were built on ash frames, fitted to chassis supplied by Montgomery's of Coventry, and were priced under £30 ($150). They were also aerodynamic, which was proven at the Isle of Man Tourist Trophy race in 1924 when motorcycles fitted with Swallow sidecars finished second, third, and fourth.

By this time England did indeed have a mass–market automobile in the form of the little Austin Seven, so named for the number of horsepower its engine provided (and could be taxed for). Lyons and Walmsley had their eye on the Seven when they moved their company to larger quarters on Cocker Street in 1926 and renamed it the Swallow Sidecar and Coach Building Company, for Lyons knew they could build a custom–bodied version of the rather plain Seven and sell it at not too expensive a price.

A chassis was bought for $560 in 1927, and Lyons gave it a two–seat sports body with a hinged top. A large Austin dealer, Henley's of London, ordered 500 of the cars, ensuring success for the new venture.

By 1928 a four–door saloon had joined the Swallow family, and the company indicated its future intent by simplifying its name to the Swallow Coachbuilding Company. That November, the company moved to Foleshill, near Coventry, England. Coventry was the center of the English automotive industry; Lyons and Walmsley were signifying their intent to be an influential presence in that industry.

The SS 1 Airline was an extremely stylish automobile, with the rear coachwork featuring a curved rear roof and a pillarless window treatment.

Swallow expanded their operations to include cars built on chassis provided by Fiat, Standard, Swift, Morris, Wolseley, and Austin. Lyons persuaded the managing director of Standard, John Black, to sell a modified version of Standard's six–cylinder chassis, and with this, Swallow's first total car design, the SS 1, was created. What "SS" stood for has never been proven—"Swallow Sports" or "Standard Swallow" seem the most likely candidates—but with its long hood and low–slung lines, the car proved a sensation. Journalists dubbed it "The Car With the Thousand–Pound Look," but it sold for only $1,550.

It was not a fast car, initially. The 16–hp 2–liter Standard engine meant the car took over 20 seconds to achieve 50 mph, and its top speed, when in tune, might reach 70 mph. The SS 1, however, looked as though it could run with the best of the period, which certainly contributed to its success.

The original fixed–head coupe was joined in 1933 by a four–seat convertible, the Tourer, which also had a fold–down windscreen and cutaway doors.

Later that year Lyons totally redesigned the SS 1 on a new chassis that was 7 inches longer in its wheelbase. The Standard engine was enlarged

into 2.1– and 2.6–liter variants (with output of 53 and 68 hp, respectively), and the body was updated with a larger passenger compartment, revised instrumentation, a better–proportioned roof, and swept–back wings (fenders).

For 1934 a new model, the Four–Light Saloon, joined the line. Its specifications were identical to the coupe, but the dummy hood irons on the side of the roof were replaced with an additional window on each side, which made the interior feel less cramped, particularly for rear–seat passengers.

The following year two additional variants, the Airline and a drophead coupe, expanded the SS 1 line to five models. The Airline was an extremely stylish automobile, with the rear coachwork featuring a curved rear roof and a pillarless window treatment. The drophead offered the integrity and comfort of a saloon car, offering wind–up windows, while having a lined, fully retractable top that could fold away and disappear under the hinged trunk lid.

Simultaneous to the release of the SS 1 was a four–cylinder version, the SS 2. Its smaller engine made for a shorter hood, making it nowhere near as pretty a car as the SS 1. It was only two–thirds the price of the SS 1, however, providing a distinctive package for the motorist who didn't need the size or performance of the larger car.

It too received substantial modifications in 1933, including a new chassis with a wheelbase fully 13 inches longer than that of the original, allowing it to become a four–seat car. It also benefited from styling changes similar to those made to the SS 1.

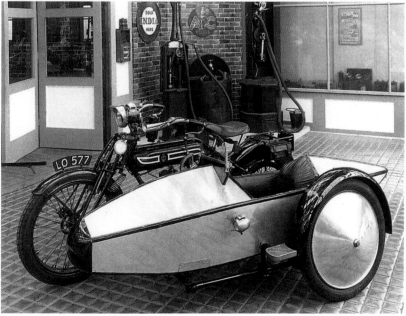

Jaguar's legacy grew from the Swallow Sidecar Company, a joint venture between William Lyons and William Walmsley, motorcycle enthusiasts with an eye for design.

The Sporting Life

When the SS 90 was introduced by SS Cars Limited in March 1935, it was the company's first true sports car, with the designation indicating the car's top speed. Mechanically identical to the SS 1, it was built on a shortened chassis, while the 2.6–liter straight six was fitted with twin RAG carburetors, giving it an output of 70 hp.

Yet after only 23 units of the SS 90 were built, it gave way to a much–improved version, the SS 100. The chassis benefited from Burman worm steering and Girling rod brakes, while an improved cylinder head, designed by Weslake, and twin SU carburetors boosted output to 104 hp. The car was fitted with a Le Mans–style rear fuel tank, upon which a pair of spare wheels was mounted at a rakish angle. The appearance of the two–seater was simple, purposeful, and elegant, the very epitome of 1930s sports car design. It differed from the SS 990 in having new headlights and a revised recessed grill, where on top of the radiator was the inscription, "SS Jaguar."

Between the introduction of these two sports models, Lyons had been busy trying to come up with a new name for his cars. "Sunbeam" had been considered, but Rootes, a company later to gain fame for the manufacture of super-chargers owned rights to the name. "Jaguar" was chosen after permission was granted by aircraft engine manufacturer Armstrong–Siddley, another Coventry operation that named its products after big cats.

The SS 100 was fitted with a Le Mans–style rear fuel tank, upon which spare wheels were mounted at a rakish angle. It remains one of the most success-fully realized sports car designs of the age.

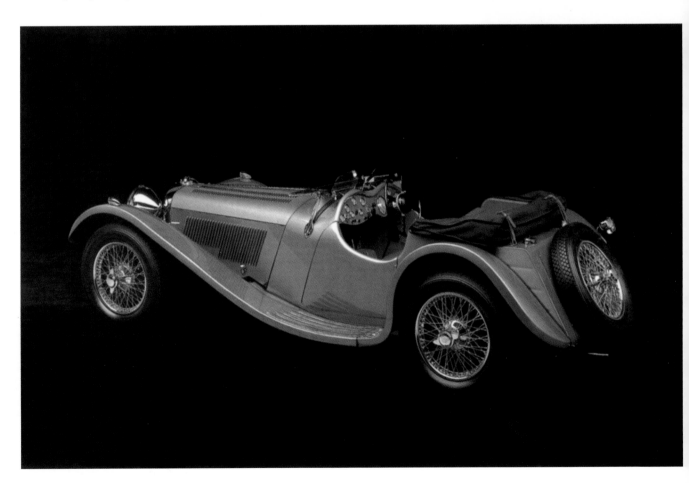

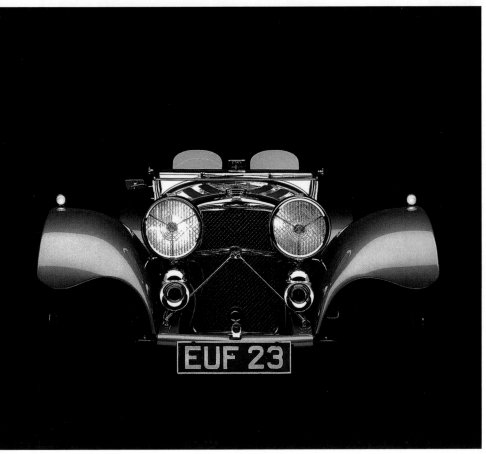

The chassis of the SS 100 benefited from Burman worm steering and Girling rod brakes, while an improved cylinder head, designed by Weslake and twin SU carburetors provided output of 104 hp.

The appearance of the two–seater SS 100 was simple, purposeful and elegant, the very epitome of 1930s sports car design.

*For the 1938 model
year, a stiffer chassis
was introduced for
the SS 100, along with
a 3.5–liter engine, based
on a Standard unit
and redesigned by SS.*

For the 1938 model year, a stiffer chassis was introduced for the SS 100, along with a 3.5–liter engine, based on a Standard unit and redesigned by SS. It featured a multiple–branch exhaust manifold and a seven–bearing crankshaft, providing 125 hp at 4,250 revolutions per minute (rpm). Together with a higher rear axle ratio of 3.8:1, the SS 100 could reach 60 mph in 10.4 seconds and had a top speed of 101 mph.

Simultaneously, a new saloon line was launched. Accolades from the automotive press included this comment from *Motor* magazine: "With distinguished appearance, outstanding performance and attractive price as the main characteristics, the new SS Jaguar range represents an achievement of which Mr. Lyons and his technical staff may well feel proud."

Dials in the SS 100 had black–on–white faces, with separate speedometer and tachometer. Thanks to its 3.5–liter, six–cylinder engine, it could indeed reach the top speed of 100 mph the speedo indicated.

*A 1939 SS Jaguar 1.5–liter saloon. These
stalwart sedans were offered through 1948.*

Available in 1.5- and 2.5-liter versions (with the four- and six-cylinder engines, respectively), the SS Jaguar saloons were based on a modified SS 1 chassis, but their hallmark was their distinguished and advanced styling. Similar in appearance to the Bentleys of the time, they were well-proportioned cars with a prominent radiator, Lucas P100 headlamps, a boot (trunk) area integrated into the tail, and a strip of chrome trim along the waistline. They were also significantly larger than the SS 1: the six-cylinder car was 14 feet, 10 inches long.

Inside, the SS Jaguar saloons were luxuriously appointed with pleated leather seating, prodigious use of walnut veneers, space for five, a sliding metal sunroof, an adjustable steering column, and a very nifty tool kit built in to the boot lid. Later improvements included opening front quarter-windows, a separate wiper motor, larger brake drums, improved carburation and air cleaning, and an automatic choke.

For sheer purposefulness, one can't beat the front view offered by the SS 100. This is a 1938 model.

The rear wheels of the Mark V were fitted with wheel covers, which added to the grace and harmony of the car's lines.

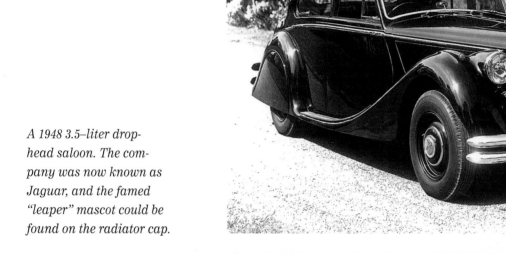

A 1948 3.5–liter drop-head saloon. The company was now known as Jaguar, and the famed "leaper" mascot could be found on the radiator cap.

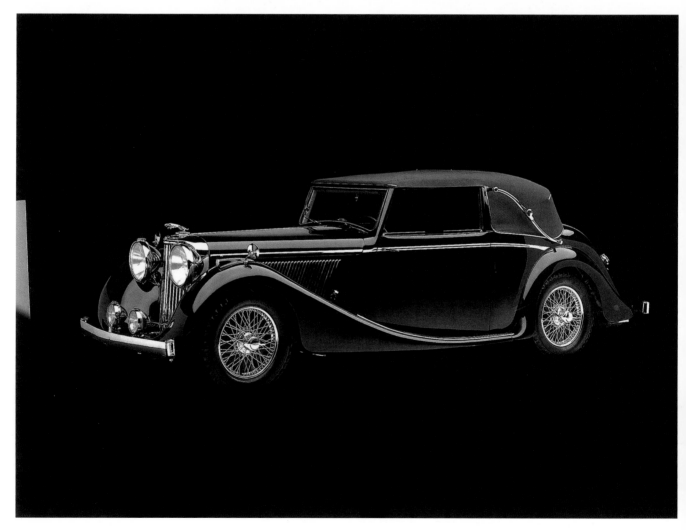

Demand for the line was quite high, which stressed the company's ability to turn out the car's alloy and steel body panels, which were mounted on an ash frame. An all–steel body was fitted, which, being 8 inches longer, made the cars look even sleeker. The length all went to the wheelbase, making the car even roomier. After 1938, the 3.5–liter engine also used in the SS 100 was available.

Although automobile production was suspended during World War II, the engineers of what would soon be known as Jaguar Cars Limited were busy coming up with new designs for engines, chassis, and front suspension. The SS Jaguars went back into production for two years after hostility ceased, but postwar shortages delayed the introduction of new technology. To keep customer interest intact, an interim saloon, the Mark V, bowed in 1948.

The Mark V had new styling reminiscent of the prewar SS Jaguar saloons, and continued to use the Standard–based six–cylinder engines. The new chassis and front suspension designs did find their way into the new car, and all–steel wheels were used for the first time. As wire–wheel knockoff spindles were no longer necessary, the rear wheels were fitted with wheel covers, which added to the grace and harmony of the car's lines, which were best appreciated from a rear three–quarter view.

A slightly larger and heavier car than its predecessor, the Mark V was also somewhat slower, but the stiff, box–section chassis members and the independent, wishbone front suspension greatly improved driving characteristics. A two–door drophead coupe was also offered that, although it was more labor–intensive to build, sold at the same price as the saloon.

While stately and elegant, the Mark V's drivability made it popular with rally drivers. The cars came in third and ninth at the 1951 Monte Carlo Rally, and third in class in the Royal Automobile Club Rally the following year.

The Mark V had new styling reminiscent of the prewar SS Jaguar saloons, and continued to use the Standard–based six–cylinder engines. This is a drophead coupe.

FOLLOWING PAGE: Built with Le Mans in mind, the D–type was mechanically similar to its predecessor, except that the engine was lubricated by the dry–sump method, allowing it to be placed lower in the frame and thus improving the car's aerodynamic potential.

The XK–120 roadster was the first Jaguar to use an engine of the company's own design.

A 1953 XK–120 drophead coupe offered improved comfort over the roadster, but somewhat compromised the orignal's style.

The Birth of the XK

The new engine that had been developed was finally unveiled in October 1948 at the London Motor Show. Both the 3.4–liter, six–cylinder engine and the aluminum–bodied roadster it appeared in were unlike anything the automotive world had ever seen. The engine had dual overhead camshafts in an all–aluminum head with hemispherical combustion chambers, a seven–bearing counterbalanced crankshaft, twin SU carburetors, and a lightweight cast–iron block. This "XK" engine even looked speedy, thanks to its polished alloy cam covers. It was rated at 160 hp.

The styling of the new roadster, dubbed the XK–120 in a projection of what its top speed would be, featured a sleek and integrated fender line and rear wheel covers reminiscent of the Mark V saloon as part of its hand–made aluminum body. A simple oval radiator grill was integrated into the hood, giving the engine bay the appearance of a gaping alligator's maw when opened.

Never intended for anything but limited production, the huge demand for the sleek roadster embarrassed Lyons and company to give up on hand–made aluminum bodies for the efficacies of mass production in steel. This facilitated the introduction of a fixed–head coupe in March 1951, which had a profile quite similar to the company's Mark V saloon cars, along with a striking resemblance to the Bugatti Atlantic, a design Lyons was known to have admired. By that autumn wire wheels became available, along with a special–order cylinder head that boosted engine output to 180 hp. A drophead coupe, the rarest of all XK–120s was introduced in the spring of 1953.

The 34–liter six, conceived by William Lyons while on fire-watch duty during the Second World War, would be the heart and soul of Jaguars for more than 40 years. It propelled the XK–120 to a 120 mph top speed.

The XK–120's interior was luxurious by sports car standards, with leather seats and dash, full instrumentation and carpeting.

The cars were very successful in road races of the period, and this success spurred Jaguar to develop a purpose–built sports racer, the C–type. The car featured a special cylinder head for the XK engine that provided 220 hp and was built on a space–frame chassis made of steel tubing, fitted with an independent rear suspension. Malcolm Sayer designed its hand–built, aerodynamic body. Its first assault on the 24 Hours of Le Mans was a smashing success, with a C–type driven by Peter Walker and Peter Whitehead winning at an average speed of 93.5 mph.

Cooling problems stemming from a body redesign forced all three team cars out of the following year's Le Mans competition, but things werefixed for 1953.With disc brakes, lighter equipment, engine performance upgrades, and redesigned rear suspensions, the cars finished first, second, fourth, and ninth, with the team of Tony Rolt and Duncan Hamilton winning. The company ultimately would supply C–types to private buyers; they achieved production status at the factory and had their own sales brochure.

Meanwhile, a successor to the C–type was under development. Built with Le Mans in mind, the D–type was mechanically similar to its predecessor, except that the engine was lubricated by the dry–sump method, allowing it

Malcolm Sayer again designed the bodywork for the D–type that, thanks to considerable wind–tunnel testing, was very advanced for the time, creating a shape that has become a classic.

to be placed lower in the frame and thus improving the car's aerodynamic potential. Sayer again designed the bodywork that, thanks to considerable wind–tunnel testing, was very advanced for the time, creating a shape that has become a classic.

The nose's streamlined shape featured faired–in headlights and a grilless mouth to facilitate engine cooling. A metal divider separated the driver's and passenger's seats, which were respectively detailed with a wrap–around Perspex windscreen and metal tonneau cover. At the rear, a long tailfin was faired in behind the driver's head (although some units would ultimately receive a cut–down, rounded fin).

Bowing at Le Mans in 1954, a D–type finished second and would have won were it not for reliability problems. Victory did come in 1955, albeit at a horrible price: the leading Mercedes–Benz team withdrew after the tragic Pierre Levegh/Lance Macklin accident that killed 80 spectators, handing the win to Jaguar. D–types did win Le Mans outright the following two years in the hands of the Scottish racing team, Ecurie Ecosse.

The D–type would ultimately influence production Jaguars. Indeed, a road–going D–type called the XKSS was developed to use up spare monocoques at the factory. The tailfin, passenger separation, and tonneau cover were removed, while a luggage rack, folding top, chrome quarter–bumpers, and Ford Consul windscreen were fitted, creating one of the fastest production sports cars in the world. But the February 1957 fire limited production to only 16 units. The D–type's influence would be most seen in the development of the fantastic E–type, as the next chapter illustrates.

The company's first assault on the 24 Hours of Le Mans was a smashing success, with a XK–120–based C–type driven by Peter Walker and Peter Whitehead winning at an average speed of 93.5 mph.

The Jaguar XJ

New features in the Mark V included independent front suspension and hydraulic brakes. The chassis would serve as the basis for the later Mark VII.

CHAPTER TWO

GROWTH WITH GRACE

The Mark VII saloon, introduced in 1950, was Jaguar's first family car to be constructed completely from componentry of original design. The styling was evolutionary, yet it was a much larger car than the Mark V, being 9 inches longer, 4 inches wide, and 1 inch taller. Priced at only a third of a comparable Bentley, the Mark VII was an instant success, with great numbers of orders coming in from North America.

Despite its large size, the Mark VII offered levels of performance and handling found in sports cars, and like its predecessor, it proved a formidable competitor in rallies and saloon car races.

The most significant update the car received was in September 1954, when the Mark VIIM variant was introduced. Revised camshafts boosted horsepower to 190, which provided a top speed of 105 mph, a speed the car could handle with ease, thanks to larger gearbox ratios and thicker torsion bars, which reduced body roll in the turns.

When production of the Mark VII concluded in July 1957, more than 30,000 cars had been produced. After October 1956, it was joined by the Mark VIII, based on the same styling but equipped with a new "B" type cylinder head and other engine modifications that boosted torque and increased horsepower to 210.

The Mark VIII had some relatively minor, but still significant, styling updates. A single curved unit replaced the two-piece windscreen, while the front grill was now notably surrounded with chrome. Finally, "the Leaper," a chromium Jaguar mascot of the big cat, was now found on the front of the hood. Inside, rear–seat passengers now could enjoy fold-away picnic tables, made of wood veneer, which folded into the seat in front of them.

The car had some interesting mechanical modifications. The Borg & Warner automatic transmission option now came with a "speed hold" switch that prevented the box from changing gears needlessly during vigorous driving. Some cars also came equipped with a power steering system that would be standard equipment on the Mark IX, which bowed in 1958.

Rear passengers of the Mark IX got to enjoy veneered picnic tables and a magazine rack.

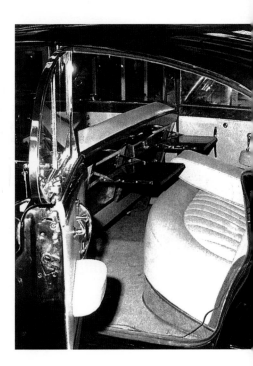

The big news in the Mark IX was the fact that the engine had been bored out to 3.8 liters and now produced 220 hp. The brakes were upgraded to four–wheel disc units made by Dunlop. The Mark IX continued in production until 1961, with a total of slightly more than 10,000 cars constructed.

Jaguar's original sports car designs were also undergoing development, as seen at the launch of the XK–140. Given a lack of development time and pressures on production facilities, the company chose to upgrade the XK–120, instead of replacing it. The car now had 190 hp available, which became 210 hp with the C–type cylinder head fitted. An improved cooling system was fitted, along with overdrive for the transmission, Alford & Alder rack–and–pinion steering, better front springs, and Girling telescopic shock absorbers.

The engine had been moved forward 3 inches, giving the XK–140 a roomier interior that featured a small rear seat, best used by children facing punishment. The increased length meant that the fixed–head coupe, unfortunately, was not as pretty a car as it once was. Bodywork on the XK–140 was very similar to that of the XK–120, but featured increased use of chrome on hood and boot trim and the radiator grill. Heavier bumpers with protectors were also installed. A plaque on the boot lid boasted of the company's racing success at Le Mans.

The cozy quarters of the XK–150 fixed–head coupe. The interior benefited from more comfortable seating and a new dashboard that was faced with leather and had a roll added to the top.

*With the Mark IX, capacity of the XK engine had been boosted to
3.8 liters. Brakes were now four-wheel disc units. This is a 1960 model.*

Idyllically posed by an English canal is this 1959 XK–150 drophead coupe. After 1960, a larger 3.8–liter engine became available, which provided 220 hp in standard trim.

The XK–150 updated the look of the Jaguar sports car, offering a wider grill, a raised body wing line, and a full wrap–around rear bumper.

In its three years of existence only 9,051 XK–140s were produced. They served to keep customer interest in the model line alive while a more advanced XK was developed—the XK–150.

Initially offered in only fixed–head and drophead coupe styles when introduced in May 1957, the XK–150 updated the look of the Jaguar sports car, offering a wider grill, the raising of the body wing line, and a full wrap–around rear bumper. This created a more substantial–looking automobile that also looked more up–to–date, particularly when one noted the new one–piece windscreen.

The interior benefited from more comfortable seating and a new dashboard that was faced with leather and had a roll added to the top. Thinner doors provided driver and passenger with considerably more elbow room.

A roadster was introduced in March 1958. It had no rear seats, its Mohair top could fold away out of sight, and the rear bodywork carried forward to the rear of the two seats, creating a particularly long, low, and sleek appearance.

An "S" engine option was soon made available that raised horsepower to 250, due to new Weslake cylinder heads, a trio of 2–inch SU carburetors, new intake and exhaust manifolds, a lighter flywheel, and a 9:1 compression ratio. With all this power, stopping ability was improved with disc brake pads developed from the D–type racing model.

After 1960, a larger 3.8–liter engine became available, which provided 220 hp in standard trim or 265 hp in "S" configuration; this latter car proved very popular in the American market.

The final XK–150 ceased production in 1961, marking the end of the XK line, as well as the end of traditional frame–chassis sports cars at Jaguar.

West Coast American styling influences, as interpreted by the Italian styling house Ghia, which managed to get its hands on an XK–150 chassis.

A Mid-Sized Saloon

By the mid–1950s, Jaguar had realized that the market for saloon cars might easily accommodate something smaller than it normally produced, so in 1956, after £100,000 in development costs, its first small saloon, the 2.4–liter, was launched. Jaguar's first car of monocoque construction (where the body shell and chassis are constructed as a single unit), what soon was known as the Mark 1 had frontal styling themes reminiscent of the XK–140, plus a single, swooping beltline, four doors, and a shorter–stroke version of the venerable XK engine. Its sinuous appearance was enhanced by a rear track that was 4.25 inches narrower than that at the front.

This smaller car was no less luxurious than its larger siblings. Leather covered separate bucket seats in manual–transmission Mark Is, or a one–piece bench front seat in automatic cars. There was a walnut–veneer dashboard and interior window surrounds, and in the Special Edition model, a comprehensive array of instrumentation and switchgear.

The success of the 2.4–liter car compelled Jaguar to roll out a 3.4–liter version for 1957, which hit factory showrooms that March despite the factory fire of the previous month. The car boasted a larger radiator and clutch, and a twin exhaust system; an automatic transmission was also available.

The updated Mark II rolled out in 1959, which featured an airier cabin thanks to thinned–down window frames and a larger rear window, and a rear track widened by 3.25 inches. The mechanical news was that the car was now available with the XK engine in 2.4–, 3.4– and 3.8–liter sizes.

The Mark II, with its unique, drawn–in rear quarters, represented a new, smaller Jaguar sedan. This is a 1962 3.8–liter model.

Improved Mark IIs were introduced in 1959; among the changes were standard fog lamps, fitted in place of the original air intakes.

Ads of the time touted the Mark II as being "Responsive as a sports car yet meticulously fitted with all the appurtenances of supreme comfort.

The Mark II remained in production for seven years, with major modifications happening in September 1965 (a fully synchromeshed four–speed transmission was made available) and in 1967, when a variable power steering system was offered. In line with the company's model designation policy, the models were renamed the 240 and 340 in September 1967, and they remained in production through 1969. A total of more than 128,000 of the Mark I/II and 240/340 models were made during their seven–year run.

FOLLOWING PAGE: A 1967 3.4–liter Mark II saloon. As of September 1965, a four–speed, all–synchromesh gear-box, already fitted on the Mark X and E–type, became standard.

Under a new nomencla-ture system, 3.4–liter Mark IIs were known as the 340 sedan during its final two years of production: 1967–68.

Getting Modern

As the 1960s were getting under way, Jaguar desperately needed some new products, since the Mark IX saloon, as a design, was getting long in the tooth. The company adapted monocoque construction for its large saloon cars, a process first manifested in the imposing Mark X, introduced in October 1961.

In appearance a thoroughly modern car, one that was much lower and sleek-er than the Mark IX, the new Mark X was the largest Jaguar yet produced, being 16 feet, 10 inches long and 6 feet, 4 inches wide. It retained some tradi-tional Jaguar styling cues, such as a sloping boot lid, traditional radiator grill, and chrome window frames, but the rest of the car was all new. It featured a lowered hood line and a slimmer grill that was swept forward, which made the hood line appear even less high. It also had four headlights, and smaller 14–inch wheels (compared to the 16–inch wheels found on the Mark IX), which made the Mark X appear even more imposing.

In appearance a thorough-ly modern car, one that was much lower and sleeker than the Mark IX, the Mark X was the largest Jaguar yet produced, being 16 feet, 10 inches long and 6 feet, 4 inches wide.

Life with Daimler

Jaguar had inherited some ongoing designs from the Daimler company when they purchased the operation in 1960. These included the SP250, a fiber glass–bodied, V–8 powered sports car that remained in production until 1964. The engine, at 2.5 liters, was a little jewel, making comprehensive use of aluminum and proving smooth and quiet in operation, all the while developing 140 hp.

Jaguar's engineers saw potential in the engine and ultimately used it to power a variant of the Mark II saloon called the Daimler 2.5–liter V–8 saloon. This model started a Jaguar tradition of developing upmarket variants of their own product and badging them as Daimlers.

The E–type, a Malcolm Sayer design, was powered by a 265–hp version of the XK engine and had lines that recalled the D–type racing machine.

Welcome the E-type

An all–new and lusty sports car, the E–type proved to be an instant success after its introduction at the Geneva Salon in March 1961. This Malcolm Sayer design, powered by a 265–hp version of the XK engine, had lines that recalled the D–type racing machine. It was introduced as a roadster and as a fixed-head, fastback coupe, and the public just fell in love with the latter.

Sleek and impressive–looking at speed (which could reach 151 mph), the E–type fastback also looked imposing at rest, opened up. The entire nose

*Sleek and impressive–looking at speed (which could
reach 151 mph), the E–type also looked imposing at rest.*

A 1961 E–type fastback. An all–new and lusty sports car, the E–type proved to be an instant success after its intro- duction at the Geneva Salon in March 1961.

tipped forward to show off the three–carburetor, dual–overhead–cam engine, while the back door opened on a side hinge to provide entry to a cavernous storage compartment.

For suspension, the front end had dual wishbones and torsion bars, while the rear was all–new, mounted on a sub–frame with two pairs of coil springs and uni- versal half–shafts, located by radius arms and transverse links. Telescopic shock absorbers and Dunlop disc brakes were found at all four wheels, with the rear brakes being mounted on the inside of the rear axle, next to the differential.

After 1965, the E–type received the 4.2–liter XK engine, a new badge on the trunk lid and more comfortable seats.

The 3.8–liter engine found in competition E-types of 1961–62. It could produce upwards of 344 hp.

The most expensive Jaguars ever

The entire nose of the E–type tipped forward to show off the three–carbure-tor, dual–overhead-cam engine, which produced 265 hp.

This is the E-type Jaguar that wowed the crowds with its introduction at the 1961 New York Auto Show.

A 1966 E–type fastback. After 1965, the E-type received the 4.2–liter XK engine, a new badge on the trunk lid and more comfort- able seats.

This 1970 Series II E–type convertible shows some of the changes made after 1965. The seating offers more comfort, and the wrap around bumpers are considerably stronger than before.

A new E-type variant came out in March 1966, the 2+2, which featured a rear seat usable by a pair of children, or an adult willing to sit sideways. The roofline was raised two inches to provide some headroom in the rear.

The 15-year production run of the E-type saw many efforts to make the car comply with safety regulations promoted by the United States government. Late in 1967, the lovely glass fairings over the headlights were removed, and dashboard toggle switches were replaced by rockers. The Series II E-type, introduced the following year, had headlights that had been moved forward somewhat, along with sturdier bumpers. The little "earflaps" that had graced wire-wheel knockoffs since the beginning were removed. Pollution regulations resulted in the SU carburetors being replaced by Zenith-Strombergs, which cut output down to 246 hp.

But William Lyons and company had one more idea that would address the E-type's power crisis, as we shall see.

A 1969 Series II fast-back E-type. Lovely and capacious, the fastback was universally loved.

The sole E–type in the line as of 1971 was the
Series III V–12 2+2, with its longer wheelbase.

CHAPTER THREE

A HERITAGE RENEWED

For years it had been rumored that Jaguar was working on a V–12 engine, which the Coventry concern indeed had, ever since 1966, though it did its best to hide the fact. The project had its infancy in the XJ–13 racing prototype, a design that resembled Ford GT40s and Lolas of the era and was perhaps the single most beautiful car Jaguar ever produced. The XJ–13 never raced because it crashed during development, but not before sufficient test data on its 5.0– liter, V–12 all–aluminum engine had been acquired. After four years of development, a 5.0–liter version found its way into the production E–type. Meanwhile, Jaguar continued to deny that the XJ–13 ever existed, until the company decided to restore the vehicle for promotional purposes.

When the Series III E–type bowed in March 1971, it was fitted with the new engine, which developed 314 hp, or almost one horsepower per cubic inch. The sole model in the line was now the 2+2, with its longer wheelbase. Stylistically, the car's windshield was less raked, and the air intake was larger, with a chrome grill over it for the first time.

The E–type had changed radically over its 15–year lifetime. It had become bigger and heavier, yet it still retained its panache. Production ended in 1975, three years after William Lyons resigned from Jaguar.

As the company continued to expand during the 1960s, it recognized other opportunities in the saloon market, particularly for a luxury car neither as large as the Mark X nor as sporty as the Mark II. The fruit of this realization were designated the S–type (produced from 1963 to 1968) and the 420 (1966–1969).

Stylistically, the rear end of the car resembled the Mark X, the passenger section was very similar to that of the Mark IPs, while the front end received an all–new treatment. New shaping to the front wings incorporated eyelids over the headlights, while the fog/spot lights

The XJ–13 racing prototype was an experimental platform for the company's V–12 engine; the single model was all but destroyed in a testing accident and not renovated for a number of years, until Jaguar was ready to admit its existence.

were recessed and repositioned to the inside of the headlights. The grill received a more prominent center vane and greater use of chrome.

Mechanically, the engine, transmission and front axle were from the Mark 2, while the rear suspension came from the E–type. The end result was a car that offered a more comfortable ride than the Mark 2, yet promised more economy, agility, and less bulk than the Mark X. More than 25,000 units of the S–type were produced of a car that was very much a transitory styling exercise for Jaguar.

The S–type provided the foundation for yet another niche product from Jaguar, the 420. Positioned between the S–type and the Mark X, the 420 was equipped with the 4.2–liter engine (as opposed to the 3.4– ad 3.8–liter units found in the S–type). The front end more resembled its big brother, having flatter front wings and four headlights.

By the early seventies, the E–type had grown into a very different type of cat indeed: this is a 1971 Series III convertible, powered by a 5.0-liter, 314–hp, V–12 engine.

The V–12 allowed the E–type to retain its sporting character in the face of American clean–air mandates.

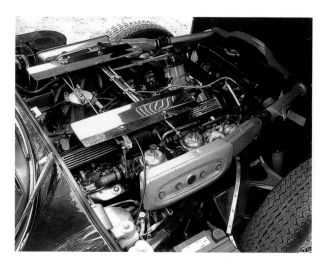

Stylistically, the Series III E–type's windshield was less raked, and the air intake was larger, with a chrome grill over it for the first time.

Sporting Yet Traditional

Jaguar's desire to find niche markets for its saloons soon waned, particularly in the light of a need to rationalize production efficiencies. This concern, and a need for an entirely modern and new saloon model, led to the introduction of the XJ series in 1968.

The first XJ6 (the Daimler equivalent was the Sovereign I) bowed that October at the Earls Court Motor Show, and proved to be such a well–thought–out, lovely design that it received Car of the Year honors. The body, while still looking like a Jaguar, was all new. The front carried over themes found in the 420, but the grill's vertical bars and heavy use of chrome were now history, as soon would be the "Leaper" hood ornament, a concession to American safety obsessionists. The roof line was squared off somewhat, and glass area greatly increased. The rear trunk panel was flat, meeting the edges of the rear wings in a flared fashion, creating a distinctive shape.

Engine offerings included 2.8– and 4.2–liter units, driving a four–speed all–synchromesh gearbox, with or without overdrive. Suspension bits were developed from existing models, with the inclusion of rubber mounting bushings to minimize noise, vibration and harshness.

A major extension to the line came in July 1972, when the XJ12/ Daimler Double Six variant, using the V–12 found in the E–type, was introduced. The car required some beefing up to handle the heavier, more powerful engine, which could drive the XJ12 to a 140 mph top speed, at the expense of single–digit fuel economy.

FOLLOWING PAGE:
The Series II XJ–12's production run totalled 22,606 cars from 1973–79. Series II build quality was becoming suspect under British Ley-land's stewardship.

This 1975 Series II XJ6C two–door hard-top coupe differed from the standard sedan by being four inches shorter and by elimination of the central door pillars.

All Jaguar XJ coupes came with a black vinyl roof. The "leaper" mascot hood ornament, by now, had become a temporary casualty of insurance insecurities.

Safety standards, particularly in the U.S., continued to evolve; meeting them successfully meant Jaguar needed an all–new XJ. The Series II, which rolled out at the Frankfurt Motor Show in August 1973, was mechanically similar to Series I cars, with some minor refinements to the heating and exhaust systems to meet environmental standards. Structurally, the Series II represented all–new cars, adding side impact beams to the doors, as well as a redesigned front end to meet bumper height standards: the front grill's depth was reduced, and below the bumper, the under–grill received a prominent chromium treatment.

Internally, ergonomic features were improved, with all gauges being situated directly in front of the driver, and the confusing array of switches being replaced with steering wheel stalk controls. XJ6s were equipped with the trusty 4.2–liter six (a 3.4–liter option was available after 1975), while XJ12s carried on with the big 5.3–liter V–12. By now, customer requests for more room were being met by a long–wheelbase edition for both models.

The Series II coupe was also available with the V–12 from 1975–77. It was good for a top speed of 147 mph. The rubber bumper facing denotes this as an American market model.

Based on a shortened XJ saloon floorpan, the new XJS was a design more of the 1970s than one reflective of Jaguar traditions—customers loved or hated it. This is a 1978 model.

The Series II line also offered a two–door coupe between 1975 and 1977 in a pillarless style. Fitted with black vinyl roofs and special "C" badging, the cars suffered from a lack of rigidity and suffered from wind noise, and water leaks. This offset their attractiveness as lighter, better performing cars, and the decision was made to cease production in November 1977.

XJs—Italian Style

The original XJ line saw its final development in the Series III saloons. The company had thought that the Series III cars would be an interim step before the all–new XJ40 saloons were launched, but their popularity was so strong that Series III models remained in production for 13 years, from 1979 to 1987 for the XJ6, and up to 1992 for the XJ12.

A 1984 XJ6 Series III model. This model, designed by Pininfarina, stayed in production for 13 years.

The line represented a new step for Jaguar, as it turned to an outside design firm for the first time in its history to update its saloons. The choice proved to be magnificent, as the company was Pininfarina, the Italian house best known for its work on Ferraris and other exotic makes.

Charged with retaining as much of the original design as possible, Pininfarina's refinements included a new, higher roof line with more vertical windscreens and greater glass area, a smoothed–out rear wing line, new energy–absorbent bumpers, reshaped wheel arches, and the return of the vertical bars to the front grill. Flush door handles were added, and front quarter windows, eliminated.

Engine choices included 3.4–, 4.2– and 5.3–liter models. The V–12 was upgraded in 1981 with a new dual–combustion chamber cylinder head that more rapidly burned lean fuel and dramatically increased fuel economy. The V–12 cars also ultimately received new GM400 automatic gearboxes, made by General Motors.

One Controversial Cat

Given the current of regulatory pressures, Jaguar felt that the true two–seat convertible sports car would be mandated out of existence. As such, the company went about developing a refined "grand touring" car as a replacement for the X–type.

Based on a shortened XJ saloon floorpan, the new XJS was a design more of the 1970s than one reflective of Jaguar traditions. Gentle curves, chrome and wood veneer were replaced by flat planes and an all matte–black interior. The only indication that this was indeed a Jaguar was the badge on the trunk lid.

Customers either loved the design or hated it. Its most controversial aspects were the rear window pillars, whose sweeping lines reminded some of the flying buttresses that held up walls of cathedrals. In fact, they were a functional, aerodynamic feature that helped the car handle strong crosswinds.

The car was initially fitted only with the V–12 engine, which provided enormous power and startling acceleration. With a top speed of over 150 mph and extraordinarily responsive handling, this new Jaguar rightfully resided in the "supercar" league; indeed, many journalists called it "the best car in the world" after it was introduced in 1975.

The "flying buttress" rear roofline on the XJS comprised aerodynamic fins that helped hold the car on the road.

"Quite possibly, the most extravagant Jaguar ever built," said ads of the XJS. Customers wondered whether this was really a Jaguar, yet it offered independent suspension, disc brakes all around, power rack–and–pinion steering, space for four, and the 5.3 liter V–12. What else could it be?

Despite its controversial aspects, the XJS had the longest shelf life–21 years–of any Jaguar model. Targa–top, convertible and six–cylinder variants (using an all–new, fuel–injected, 3.6–liter unit called the AJ–6) all surfaced during its run. The company made a huge investment in revamping the car in 1991, slimming the controversial rear window pillars, increasing glass area and adding full–width tail lights as part of the design equation.

Jaguar's saloon banner for the XJ6 and XJ12 was carried by an all–new design, code–named the XJ40, from 1986 through 1994. Six–cylinder cars carried the AJ–6 engine, allowing the company to bid a fond farewell to the XK engine and its derivatives. (The Daimler Sovereign carried the engine through 1992, giving the unit a remarkable 44–year production run.)

Among new developments in the XJ40 were the inclusion of a ZF four–speed automatic gearbox, a new rear suspension with

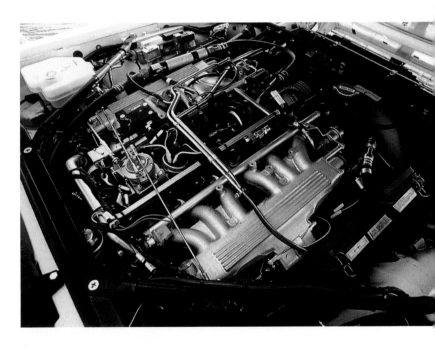

A 1995 XJS convertible. The open–air XJS out- sold its hardtop sibling by more than three to one.

The 5.3–liter V–12 engine, as found in a 1989 XJS convertible. A GM 400 three–speed automatic delivered its 285 hp to the pavement.

Despite its controversial aspects, the XJS and variants had the longest shelf life—21 years—of any Jaguar model. This is an XJR–S at speed.

After Lady Diana was said to have bought a Mercedes over a Jaguar because of the availability of a rear seat, the XJS convertible was quick to compensate.

lower wishbones and outboard–mounted disc brakes, and a self–leveling system on top-of–the–line models. The interior featured a redesigned dashboard, with instruments mounted in a central cluster.

The body shell was entirely new, a squared–off refinement justified for ease of assembly, better build–quality, easier panel replacement, and improved rust protection. But after the Pininfarina–inked lines of the Series III, the XJ40 was a bit of a disappointment.

This 1990 XJS convertible was the flagship of the line at the time. The car by now featured a Teve antilock brake system.

Supercars

Jaguar had returned to international sports car racing in the 1980s, again gaining success at Le Mans with prototypes campaigned by Tom Walkinshaw Racing (TWR). Jaguar's chief engineer, Jim Randle, had an idea about packaging the knowledge gained from racing, and soon a small team at the engineering department started developing what would be known as the XJ220, initially without the knowledge of Jaguar's board of directors.

Clad in a sensational all–aluminum tub designed by Keith Helfet, the futuristic XJ220, with its racing V–12 engine, bowed at the British Motor Show in October 1988. Reaction to the prototype was overwhelming, leading the Jaguar board, at the prodding of Tom Walkinshaw, to put the car into production.

Jaguar formed a joint company with TWR called Jaguar Sport, and three years later a production version bowed, now powered by a state–of–the–art, 3.5–liter, TWR/Jaguar engine fitted with twin turbochargers and four camshafts. This allowed the car to lay claim to being the fastest production car on earth, with an estimated top speed of over 220 mph. Three hundred and fifty of the $250,000 semi–race cars were built through 1994.

By 1994 all Jaguars offered passenger-side airbags and were prewired for cellular phones. This is an XJ12 of that year.

The engine compartment of a 1984 XJR-S, as modified by TWR. Tom Walkinshaw's group provided a range of suspension, brake, and engine modifications at customer request.

Jaguar returns to racing

The X–300, as realized in this 1995 XJ6. The X–300 represented the company's first new product since Ford provided backing.

JaguarSport also produced another race–bred prototype, the XJR–15. Based mechanically on the XJR–9 Jaguar that had won at Le Mans in 1988 but increasing its V12 engine to 6.0 liters, the car's body and chassis were constructed of Kevlar and carbon fiber. Only fifty cars were made, and all purchasers had to agree to enter the cars in a one–make racing series proposed by Tom Walkinshaw. Called the Intercontinental Series, the top prize was $1 million, races were staged as support events for Formula 1 weekends, and the factory provided support both on and off the track while the series was under way.

The XJR–15 caused some disgruntlement among XJ220 purchasers, who thought it undermined the desirability of the six–cylinder cars, even though they were 35 mph faster!

Jaguar, Present and Future

Contemporary performance sedans have had to meet an engineering and quality standard set by Japanese companies such as Lexus. Jaguar's new owner, Ford, wanted its new charge to show it could meet those standards, and with

an investment of more than $300 million developed the current XJ Series, code–named the X–300.

The new car features a much more curvaceous body than its predecessor, allowing the XJ to reclaim its roots. Modern production tooling and methods allow 11 percent less metal to be used in the body, reducing costs yet improving panel fit at the same time.

Initially offered in 1994 with two sizes of six–cylinder engines as well as the V–12, the X–300, from 1998 on, was available with a new, all-aluminum V–8 engine that offers low maintentance with 290 hp.

The XJR–15 was based mechanically on Jaguar's LeMans race winner of 1988, the XJR–9. Some felt it undermined the XJ220, having better looks, greater exclusivity and a V–12 engine, although at more than a half–million dollars it cost 20 percent more.

Despite William Lyons' belief during the 1970s that the two–seater sports car would be mandated out of existence, this has fortunately proven not to be the case. In 1996, a new two–seater, the XK8, was introduced at the Geneva Auto Salon (a coupe) and the New York Auto Show (a convertible). At the time, Nick Scheele, Jaguar's chief executive officer, said, "The XK8 reaffirms Jaguar's heritage of outstandingly beautiful sports cars. The dynamic style of the XK8 can only begin to communicate the driving experience in store."

The AJ–V8 engine offers variable valve timing off its dual overhead camshafts driving four valves per cylinder, providing smoothness and a broad range of torque accessibility. It is coupled to the company's first five–speed

FOLLOWING PAGE:
By not retracting completely, the XK8 roadster's convertible top recalls classic British sports cars of the past.

Jaguar's first V–8 engine, the AJ–V8, displaces 4.0 liters and is a work of art in its own right.

Jaguar introduced its XK8 coupe and convertible in March 1996. The line was an instant smash hit.

automatic transmission, made by ZF. The usual "J–gate" selector is coupled with two driver–selectable shift modes: "normal" and "sport." As of 1998, a supercharged version of the engine was offered, creating the XR8, distinguished by twin hood louvers and a rear spoiler.

The front suspension is an unequal–length double–wishbone design, mounted to an aluminum cross–beam that also supports the engine mounts, an arrangement that helps isolate road noise and vibration. The rear suspension is a control arm/coil spring design similar to that used in the XKR.

The car's lovely styling was created under the direction of Geoff Lawson, styling director, in such a way that the coupe design would translate easily

Jaguar's latest saloon, the XJ8, has helped the company overcome negative public perceptions for quality.

The ragtop XK8 was Jaguar's first all–new convertible design in 30 years. The top is lined and insulated with Mohair.

The business office of the XK8. The driver can select between two shift modes: normal and sport, the latter offering a performance– oriented program with gear changes timed for peak performance.

Reminiscent of the Mark II, the S–type is positioned as Jaguar's entry–level luxury sports saloon. V–6 or V–8 engines are available.

into a convertible. Bucking a current styling trend, the convertible top, which retracts automatically, is fully lined and completely soundproof, doesn't disappear into the rear of the car, but perches atop the trunk in traditional British fashion.

Always subject to modernization, Jaguars have never lost their looks, performance, or relative value to the competition. Ford's purchase of the company and investment in infrastructure should ensure that Jaguar's reputation for value should continue into the next century, which begs the question: What might future Jaguars look like?

The XK8 was designed at Whitley Engineering
Center by the late Geoff Lawson, and is about
$12,000 less expensive than the XJS it replaced.

The XK180's classic lines recall the legendary racing D–types of the 1950s.

Then there is the styling and engineering exercise called the XK180. Introduced late in 1998 at the Paris Auto Show, this non–production but fully operational prototype is based on a shortened XKR, but with all–new aluminum bodywork that brings to mind Jaguar's great roadsters of the 1950s and 1960s, particularly the D–type racing Jaguar.

As can be seen from the photos that illustrate this text, Jaguar's heritage and spirit still pervade the company, which hints that the future looked quite promising indeed.

Introduced late in 1998 at the Paris Auto Show, the XK180 is a non-production but fully operational prototype, based on a shortened XKR.

CHAPTER FOUR

LEAPING INTO THE 21ST CENTURY

Jaguar underwent a massive reorganization during the 1990s, beginning with its acquisition by Ford Motor Co. in 1990. The monumental merger ushered in a decade marked by improvements in manufacturing technology and the introduction of several new models. Those included the XJ Series in 1994, the XK8 coupe and convertible in 1996, and the V-8 XJ Series in '97. Jaguar enjoyed success on the racetrack during that period, too, with XJR-12s winning the 24-hour events at Daytona and Le Mans in 1990. Jaguar's motorsports division closed out the '90s by announcing its return to the FIA Formula One World Championship circuit. The company's connection to Britain's royal family received a boost as well when Queen Elizabeth visited its upgraded Browns Lane factory in 1994.

Jaguar left one more lasting automotive impression on the 20th century with the introduction of the much-anticipated S-Type Series mid-size luxury saloon, or sedan, for the 1999 model year. Rekindling the S-Type moniker from 1963, the new series was styled by design director Geoff Lawson (who died suddenly that same year) and produced at Jaguar's Castle Bromwich facility in Birmingham, England.

The rear-wheel-drive S-Type, reminiscent of the C-Type and Mark II, was constructed on a completely new platform shared with the Lincoln LS and Ford Thunderbird. Buyers had a choice of two engines—Jaguar's existing 4.0-liter, 281-hp V-8 or its new 3.0-liter, 240-hp V-6, both paired with a new five-speed automatic transmission. Models included a standard saloon, an SE (special equipment), Sport, and later an S-Type R. Several special editions were produced leading up to the end of production in 2007 to make way for the replacement XF models.

X-Type Marks the New Millennium

The British automaker took aim at the younger generation in 2001 with the debut of the reinvented X-Type, an entry-level competitor of the Audi A4, the BMW 3 Series, the Mercedes C Class, and the Volvo S60. Codenamed internally as the X400 and billed as "most significant new model in Jaguar's history," it borrowed structural parts from Ford, yet retained typical Jag styling and interior ambience. The X-Type was initially launched as a four-door four-seater with either a 2.5-liter or 3.0-liter V-6 engine, a choice of manual or automatic five-speed gearbox, and all-wheel drive—another first for the company. "The X-Type offers…beautiful steering and excellent road manners, a smooth and willing V-6, and a comfortable and luxurious interior," wrote Car and Driver in its first-drive review.

For 2004, Jaguar spiffed up its flagship XJ large sedan line with a third-generation model, coded the X350, featuring an all-aluminum monocoque body. The single-unit structure reduced the car's weight by 40 percent while increasing its stiffness by 60 percdent, thus improving fuel efficiency, comfort, and handling. Another new Jaguar that model year was the AKA station wagon.

The 2001 Jaguar X400 opened up a whole new audience for Jaguar cars. It combined room for a growing family with classic Jaguar elegance and style.

Jaguar shuttered its Browns Lane factory in August 2005, ending 54 years of production at the facility. Devotees of the brand still look fondly upon the venerable models that rolled off the Browns Lane line, including the XK120, the C- and D-Types, the Mark II, the E-Type, and the XJ and XJS. The occasion also marked the end of the XK8, which would be replaced the following year by the new XK, to be assembled at the Castle Bromwich site.

Jaguar showcased its latest XK model, dubbed the X150, at the 2005 Frankfurt Motor Show for the '06 model year. With sleek styling reminiscent of the fabled XK-E models of the early 1960s, yet sporting a thoroughly modern interior, the updated XK came standard with a 294-hp, 4.2-liter V-8 engine. The XK was joined by XKR coupe and convertible models a year later, powered by a supercharged V-8 that kicked out 420 hp. In 2009, the XK received a major upgrade when the engine was replaced with Jaguar's new 5.0-liter V-8 unit, both in normally aspirated and supercharged form.

In 2006, the X150 brought the two-door XKE idea of the Jaguar into a very modern age, with a powerful engine and road-ready handling.

Ta-ta Ford, Hello Tata

Jaguar underwent another major transformation in 2008, both in its vehicle design and corporate structure. Disappointed with waning Jag sales, Ford sold the company—along with its Land Rover brand, acquired from BMW in 2006—to India-based Tata Motors. Despite the front-office shakeup, Jaguar unleashed the bold new XF mid-size sedan for the 2009 model year, replacing the S-Type and X-Type sedans. Envisioned by chief stylist Ian Callum, the XF was hailed by automotive critics for its blend of futuristic and classic design, from its Aston Martin-like taillights to its '68 Jaguar XJ-inspired front grille.

Under the new cat's hood roared either a normally aspirated 4.2-liter, 300-hp V-8 or a supercharged XFR version that raised the power bar way up to 420 hp. "The XF's road manners, with its cracking power delivery, powerful brakes, and direct, well-weighted steering are a delight," Motor Trend's reviewer stated. A modified XFR set a Jaguar speed record of 225.675 mph at Utah's Bonneville Salt Flats on November 7, 2008, topping the longstanding mark of 217.1 mph set by an XJ220 in 1992.

Jaguar kept the momentum going the following year with the latest

In Jaguar sedans, the XF took over where X-Type and S-Type had gone before. Not only was it stylish as always, when modified, it put up record-breaking speeds.

The XJ sedan continued as a key part of the resurgence of Jaguar under new owners, combining elegant looks (top) with a powerful 470-hp engine (below).

iteration of its flagship XJ sedan, codenamed the X351. "The new Jaguar XJ is the epitome of fluid, contemporary automotive style," the company stated, emphasizing the elongated teardrop shape of the side windows that established the car's flowing design. The 2010 XJ introduced a variety of novel interior technologies, pioneering the use of display and infotainment systems such as the innovative Virtual Instrument dials and optional 1200W Bowers & Wilkins premium surround-sound audio.

Built on an all-aluminum body structure—comprising more than 50 percent recycled material—the XJ was available in four trim levels and two chassis versions, short and long. Several different engines, all paired with a six-speed paddle-shifted automatic transmission, were offered. Each was a variation of the 5.0-liter V-8 also found in the 2010 Jaguar XF and the XK models. The supercharged 470-hp version rocketed the XJ to 60 mph in a mere 4.9 seconds.

A Jaguar sports car? Yes! After conquering the sedan market, Jaguar moved back to its roots with the 2013 F-Type (above). The V-8 engine (opposite) rocketed to 60 mph in just 4.2 seconds, while the driver enjoyed Jaguar comfort in the convertible cabin (bottom).

Rebirth of the Two-Seater

Not since the famous E-Types of the 1960s had Jaguar produced a genuine sports car. Then along came the scintillating F-Type in 2013, described by Car and Driver's tester as "a proper two-seater with a folding fabric roof whose ancestral link to that last great Jaguar roadster is its audaciousness of spirit as much as its naming convention." Replacing the XK coupe and convertible, the F-Type shared some of their aluminum construction techniques, yet the styling was all its own. The high front end was highlighted by a wide rectangular grille and vertical bi-xenon headlights; ultra-thin taillights housed LED units. The innovative rear spoiler lifted when the car hit 60 mph, then lowered back down under 40 mph. Hidden, automatically deploying door handles were activated by either the key fob or touch-control.

The F-Type showcased new engines: a 3.0-liter supercharged V-6 in either 340-hp or 380-hp versions and a 5.0-liter supercharged V-8 in the F-Type S with 495 hp, the latter hitting 60 mph in just 4.2 seconds. All models came standard with an eight-speed transmission with paddle-shift controls, though the V-6s offered the option of a six-speed manual gearbox.

Jaguar unveiled the even more powerful F-Type SVR in 2016, both a coupe

The F-Type got faster in 2016 thanks to improved aerodynamics (below) and an even more powerful engine. The XE sedan joined the team in 2014 (opposite).

and convertible. The exterior differed from the original with wide air inlets at the front and blacked-out headlamps, roof, and rear spoiler. The V-8 was boosted to 575 hp, capable of launching the car to 60 mph in 3.5 seconds and to a top speed of 200 mph—making the SVR the first Jaguar since the XJ220 two-seater supercar of the early '90s to hit 200.

The X-Type series was updated in 2014 with the introduction of Jaguar's XE compact sedan. It was the first model using Jaguar Land Rover's new modular aluminum architecture. The car's exterior was distinguished by a shorter front overhang and a longer rear one, lending the XE a more coupe-ish shape. Sporting a nearly all-aluminum body shell, the so-called "baby Jag" was offered with a range of Ingenium four-cylinder gasoline or diesel engines, as well as the top-of-the-line 3.0-liter supercharged V-6 first seen in the F-Type sports car.

The Jaguar F-Pace

Jaguar entered the SUV market in a big way in with the F-Pace models in 2016. Using Land Rover, a cousin company, as a base, Jaguar poured in all its design know-how to the new machines.

Taking the SUV Leap

Jaguar borrowed from its Land Rover cousin to develop the British brand's very first SUV, the all-wheel-drive, diesel-powered F-Pace. Rumors of a Jaguar entry into the compact-luxury SUV market had persisted since the early 1990s during the Ford years, long before a prototype was finally rolled out at the start of the 2015 Tour de France. The finished F-Pace debuted in 2016.

Constructed around Jaguar Land Rover's D7a vehicle architecture, the chassis was nearly 80 percent aluminum, with a steel rear floor to improve front-to-rear weight distribution and steel doors. Head-on, the F-Pace resembled Jag's F-Type sedans—with squinty headlights and rectangular grille—yet its higher ground clearance, hatchback door, and overall muscularity combined for a sporty look. The interior pulled off the same look, thanks to a Sports Command driving position amidst an elegant cockpit with softly lit touchscreens and digital displays and state-of-the-art infotainment system.

Power was supplied by either a turbocharged and intercooled DOHC 16-valve diesel 2.0-liter inline-4. The eight-speed automatic transmission featured a manual-shifting mode. In test drives, the F-Pace offered exceptionally sharp on-center steering precision and great turn-in response. Jaguar's Adaptive Surface Response system automatically controlled the throttle, transmission, and stability control system to maximize traction under a variety of conditions. Dubbing it the "sports car of SUVs," Motor Trend declared the F-Pace "the enthusiast driver's choice in the SUV segment."

Jaguar announced in 2017 that it would enter the electric-vehicle market, sneak-peeking its I-Pace concept car at auto shows. However, the company's director of design Ian Callum proclaimed, "This isn't just a concept. It is a preview of a five-seat production car that will be on the road in 2018." Coincidentally, the motorsport division announced that Jaguar had entered the FIA Formula E Championship, the first all-electric international racing series. Forward thinking and race-ready: Jaguar continues to prowl.

The control panel of the conceptual I-Pace model shows that Jaguar is ready to conquer yet another market in the future: electric cars.

RESEARCH PROJECTS

1. The Jaguar automobile roams the world's highways and byways, existing on gasoline and, more recently, electricity. What about the mammal the brand is named for? Where does it live and what are some of its remarkable habits?

2. Go online and find examples of appearances by Jaguar motorcars in movies and TV shows. What characters were famous for driving one? What did it say about their roles?

3. Jaguars have evolved over the years, with new looks and new styles, but always clearly a part of the Jaguar brand. Get out your sketch books and draw some of your own Jaguars. What features would you add? What would you keep? How would you make your new Jaguar fit into the long history of the brand?

4. Where does Jaguar fit into British automaking history? Research other famous British brands and compare their output and history to Jaguar's. Perhaps you can make visual timeline of British automaking history.

FIND OUT MORE

Books

Haddock, Thomas F. with Michael C. Mueller. *Jaguar E-Type Six Cylinder Originality Guide*. Deerfield, IL: Dalton Watson, Fine Books, 2017.

Salter, Colin and Paul Walton. *Jaguar: The Iconic Models That Define the Marque*. London: Pavilion Books, 2017.

Thorley, Nigel. *Jaguar E-Type: A Celebration of the World's Favorite '60 Icon*. Poundbury, UK: Veloce Books, 2017.

Web Sites

www.jaguarusa.com

www.jaguarheritage.com

www.jec.org.uk (Jaguar Enthusiasts Club, UK)

SERIES GLOSSARY OF KEY TERMS

aerodynamics the study of how air moves over and around an object

camshaft the metal rod to which pistons are attached in a car engine

chassis the metal internal framework or skeleton of a car

coupe generally used as a term for a two-door car

endurance a type of racing that is conducted over a long time period

ergonomic designed to mold or fit a person's body shape

fuel injection a process in some car engines that sends a small amount of fuel into each of the engine's many tiny combustions

grille automotive term for the front end of a car

horsepower a measurement of engine strength, based on the power that a single horse could achieve

marque a name for an automaker's logos or car models

rpm revolutions per minute, the number of times the camshaft spins in that time period

sedan typically, a four-door car

suspension the series of springs and bars that support a car while it drives

tachometer a device that measures rpms in an engine

turbocharged describing a car engine that has additional parts that drive more air into the combustion chambers, thus increasing power of the car

transmission the set of gears that transfers power from the engine to the wheels of a car; in a manual transmission, the drivers moves a lever that makes the gears change; in automatic transmission, the car moves from gear to gear itself.

INDEX

Page numbers in **bold-face** type indicate photo captions.

INDEX

PHOTO CREDITS

Automotive Quarterly: 4-5, 6, 7, 14-15, 18, 19, 20, 26 (top & bottom), 28, 30, 31, 32, 33, 34 (top & bottom), 59 (top & bottom), 60, 74, 75 (top & bottom), 76. Jaguar Archives: 15 (bottom), 22 (top), 23, 56-57. 58, 61, 64 (top & bottom), 67 (top), 69, 78, 79. Ron Kimball: 16, 17 (top & bottom), 21, 22 (bottom), 24-25, 35, 62-63, 65, 66, 68, 70, 71, 72-73, 77. John Lamm: 27 (top & bottom), 29, 63 (right), 67 (bottom). DPP/Icon SMI/Newscom: 80. Wikimedia: 82, 83, 86, 87 (bottom), 88. Yali Shi/DT: 84. Jaguar Media Images: 85 (top & bottom), 87 (top), 88, 89. iPace interior: 90, 91.